CHARLIE
TAKES HIS SHOT

How Charlie Sifford
Broke the Color
Barrier in Golf

Nancy Churnin

pictures by
John Joven

Albert Whitman & Company
Chicago, Illinois

Verona Landis

For my husband, Michael Granberry,
with love and gratitude for your encouragement
and support as I take my shots.—NC

To God, for keeping me in the game.—JJ

Charlie positioned the golf club. Someone was coming!
If anyone saw him, he'd be in trouble.

He pulled back the club and swung. Then he ran to hide.

Charlie's ball soared pretty as a bird piercing the blue sky at dusk.

It wasn't the shot he wanted. He didn't have the time for the shot he wanted. But he grinned as his ball dove and raced on the green, skidding close to the hole.

From the moment he grasped a golf club, Charlie knew he was born to play.

It wasn't long before he could strike the ball farther and truer than anyone on the course near his home in Charlotte, North Carolina. But it was the 1930s and only white people were allowed to compcte on the private green.

So Charlie became a caddie. He lugged heavy bags of clubs while he dreamed of the day he could show off his shots for everyone to see.

He studied how players gripped their clubs and when they straightened and bent their legs and elbows.

When Charlie grew older, all that practice helped him win the tournaments black players organized for themselves on public courses.

Charlie wanted his shot at Professional Golfers' Association of America tournaments too. But those tournaments were held in private clubs that only allowed white players. No one would give him a chance to play!

WHITE ONLY

Then, in 1947 he watched Jackie
Robinson become the first black
player in Major League Baseball.
Fans taunted Jackie and told him
to go back to the cotton fields.
One of his teammates switched
teams to avoid playing with him.
But Jackie didn't quit or lose his
temper. Quietly yet powerfully, he
helped his team win by outhitting
and outrunning every opponent.

Within a year, Jackie's
teammates and fans of
every race cheered for
him. Could Charlie do
the same for golf?

In 1948 over a round of golf, Charlie got a chance to ask Jackie Robinson himself.

The baseball star thought about the question. "It's going to be awfully tough, Charlie," Jackie said finally.

He was right. On the golf courses where PGA tournaments were played, the players were white, the fans were white, and the sponsors were white. Only the caddies were black. Jackie's teammates came around when he proved his talent. But Charlie wouldn't have teammates. Golf is one person against another.

Jackie warned Charlie that people would threaten him and call him ugly names.

Charlie clenched his fist around his club. He wasn't sure he could stand that.

But Jackie told him if he stayed calm and didn't give up, he could open a door for others. "Nobody can do it but you," Jackie said.

Long after Jackie left, Charlie thought about his words. It was going to be tough, but if nobody could do it but Charlie, then Charlie was going to have to do it!

He put all his efforts into golfing, driving from New York to California and several states in between for tournaments. He became a pro, which meant that he was committed to earning his living from golf, even if some years he didn't earn much at all.

He won the National Negro Open so many times, they told him to keep the trophy! In 1957 he won $2,000 in a tournament—enough money to help him buy a house.

But no matter how well Charlie played, he couldn't get his chance at the big PGA tournaments. That's because the PGA had a "Caucasian-only" clause in their constitution, which said their members had to be white.

America was slowly tearing down the walls that kept people apart. Jackie broke the color barrier in Major League Baseball in 1947. Earl Lloyd did the same for the National Basketball Association in 1950. A Supreme Court decision led to the integration of public schools in 1954.

But in 1959 the "Caucasian-only" clause remained in golf, and Charlie couldn't figure out a way to change it.

CONSTITUTION
AND BY-LAWS

THE PROFESSIONAL GOLFERS
ASSOCIATION of AMERICA

1959

One day he picked up the *New York Post* and read a powerful column about how the PGA should let Charlie play. It was written by Jackie Robinson! People started buzzing about what Jackie said. Suddenly, Charlie felt hopeful.

In the fall of 1959 Charlie played a man who wasn't a good golfer. But Stanley Mosk was a good lawyer and a good man.

They were playing at the Hillcrest Country Club in Los Angeles, where Jewish golfers, like Stanley, had built their own club years ago when they hadn't been welcome elsewhere.

Stanley whistled at Charlie's shots as they flew, skittered and sank into cups. He asked Charlie why one of the best golfers he'd ever seen wasn't playing on the PGA tour.

"Because of this 'Caucasian' clause in their constitution," Charlie told him.

"You mean to tell me they actually have that written down as a rule?" Stanley, who was not only a lawyer, but the attorney general of California, couldn't believe how unfair that was. He promised Charlie he'd fight for his right to play.

It took two years of letters and arguments with the PGA, but Stanley's efforts got the "Caucasian-only" clause removed in 1961. Charlie became the first black player on the PGA tour!

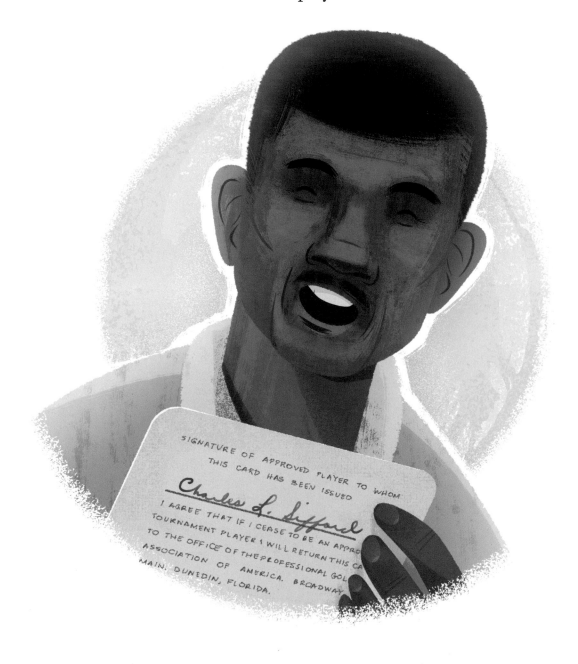

Still, Charlie's battles weren't over. Hotels where other players stayed wouldn't rent him a room. Clubs where the tournaments were held wouldn't let him eat with other players, change in their locker rooms, or use their bathrooms.

Once a stranger called him and said, "You'd better not bring yourself out to our golf course if you know what's good for you."

Another time when he went to putt his ball, someone kicked it far away.

Charlie kept going. He practiced his swing. He studied courses to figure out the right club and angle for each shot. And he tried to close his ears to the jeers of people who didn't want him there.

Then, six years after Charlie had joined the PGA tour, he noticed something different about the crowd at a tournament in Hartford, Connecticut.

For the first time, no one was rooting against him. Swing. Putt. Sink. Hole by hole, he kept advancing!

On the final hole, Charlie positioned the golf club. But Charlie rushed the way he had long ago when someone was about to chase him away.

Thunk! The ball fell down, down, down into a sand trap.
It would be a tough, if not impossible, shot.
To Charlie's surprise, he heard encouraging murmurs.

The crowd wanted him to win. They believed he could win.
Suddenly Charlie believed too.

He took out his wedge, closed his eyes, and…swoosh!

This time, the ball flew high, fluttered, and landed softly four feet from the cup.

He putted. Clink! The crowd roared and clapped for fifteen minutes.

Charlie wiped his wet eyes.

He won $20,000. It felt like a million.

Charlie did it: he had opened a door for others.

Now Charlie played golf the way he'd dreamed since he was little, showing off his shots for all to see.

And now it was possible for everyone who loved
the game to play and hear cheers from the crowd.

Author's Note

Charles Luther Sifford waged a long, lonely fight to become the first black man to break the color barrier in the Professional Golfers' Association of America in 1960.

Sifford was born in Charlotte, North Carolina, on June 2, 1922. In 1946 he married his wife, Rose, and together they had two sons, Charles Jr. and Craig. Throughout more than fifty years of marriage, Rose supported Sifford's dream of playing golf professionally, even when it seemed improbable to others and kept him away from home for long stretches of time.

Before Sifford played on the PGA Tour, he won the United Golf Association's National Negro Open so many times—from 1952 to 1956 and again in 1960—they told him to keep the trophy. He was the first black man inducted into the World Golf Hall of Fame in 2004.

Jackie Robinson, who broke the color barrier in Major League Baseball in 1947, was an inspiration, a friend, and an advocate for Sifford, going so far as to write a column for the *New York Post* urging the PGA to allow Sifford to join.

Stanley Mosk, then attorney general of California and later associate justice of the California Supreme Court, was another ally—a fierce defender of civil rights who became a good friend of Sifford's. Mosk argued Sifford's discrimination case against the PGA and won.

Once Sifford had his PGA card, it took several years to get the crowd on his side. But he did, finally, at the Greater Hartford Open, which he won in 1967. It was his first PGA Tour win, followed by wins at the Los Angeles Open in 1969 and the Senior PGA Championship in 1975.

Tiger Woods, one of the most successful golfers of all time, has credited Sifford for making his career possible, saying that without Sifford, he probably wouldn't have ever picked up the game of golf.

Sifford received an honorary doctorate from the University of St Andrews. In 2011 the Revolution Park Golf Course in Charlotte, North Carolina, where he had so much trouble finding a place to play golf growing up, was renamed the Dr. Charles L. Sifford Golf Course at Revolution Park. In 2014 President Barack Obama awarded Sifford the Presidential Medal of Freedom.

Time Line

1922 Charles Luther Sifford is born on June 2nd in Charlotte, North Carolina.

1932 Begins work as a caddie at the Carolina Country Club near his home.

1939 Moves to Philadelphia, Pennsylvania; begins playing against African American golfers.

1948 Meets Jackie Robinson at the Western Amateur Open golf tournament in Los Angeles. Robinson broke the color barrier in Major League Baseball when he played for the Brooklyn Dodgers in 1947. Sifford wonders if he can do the same for golf.

1952–1956 Wins the United Golf Association's National Negro Open every year five years, winning a sixth time in 1960.

1957 Wins the Long Beach Open, which was not an official Professional Golfers' Association of America-sanctioned event, but was cosponsored by the PGA and included white players.

1959 Meets Stanley Mosk, attorney general of California, at the Hillcrest Country Club in Los Angeles, a Jewish club that welcomed African Americans. Mosk pressures the PGA to drop their "Caucasian-only" clause, which stated that only white people could join the PGA and be eligible for the PGA Tour.

1961 Becomes the first African American golfer in the PGA. He joins the PGA Tour.

1967 Becomes the first African American golfer to win a PGA tournament, the Greater Hartford Open. Wins by one stroke.

1969 Wins the Los Angeles Open with a birdie on the first extra hole. (A birdie is one stroke under par. Par is the number of strokes a player should hit to get a ball into a particular hole.)

1975 Wins the Senior PGA Championship, the leading tournament for golfers over fifty years old.

2004 Becomes the first African American inducted into the World Golf Hall of Fame.

2006 Receives an honorary Doctor of Laws degree from the University of St Andrews.

2007 Receives the Old Tom Morris Award, which is the Golf Course Superintendents Association of America's highest honor.

2009 The Northern Trust Open creates the Charlie Sifford Exemption in his honor enabling a player who represents the advancement of diversity in golf to compete.

2011 Mecklenburg County Park and Recreation in Sifford's native Charlotte, North Carolina, changes the name of Revolution Park Golf Course to Dr. Charles L. Sifford Golf Course at Revolution Park.

2014 President Barack Obama awards Sifford the Presidential Medal of Freedom.

2015 Sifford dies on February 3rd at the age of ninety-two.

Acknowledgements

I would like to thank my wonderful editor, Wendy McClure, and my agent, Karen Grencik, for finding Charlie such a terrific home. I would also like to thank the great Dan Jenkins for his encouragement, kindness, and generosity in sharing his personal knowledge of Charlie Sifford. My deep appreciation, too, goes to Dr. Tony Parker, historian at the World Golf Hall of Fame; Laury Livsey, senior director, PGA Tour History, and Bob Denney, PGA of America historian for fact-checking the story. Thank you, most of all, to Charlie Sifford, who fought a long, difficult fight with grace so that he could leave a better and fairer world to all children, including my own beloved boys, Ted, Sam, David, and Josh Granberry.

Library of Congress Cataloging-in-Publication data is on file with the publisher.

Text copyright © 2018 by Nancy Churnin
Pictures copyright © 2018 by John Joven
Published in 2018 by Albert Whitman & Company
ISBN 978-0-8075-1128-2

Printed in China
10 9 8 7 6 5 4 3 2 1 LP 22 21 20 19 18 17

Design by Jordan Kost

For more information about Albert Whitman & Company,
visit our website at www.albertwhitman.com.